K. Hardison
THE VISIONS OF THE CLOSED EYED DELICACY

This book is dedicated to all my Sisters who have weathered the storms in life by staying focused and connected to God!!

K. Hardison
THE VISIONS OF THE CLOSED EYED DELICACY

Acknowledgements

To JESUS: …. for making all things possible!!!

To my family, thank you for always encouraging me and pushing me into my Destiny! Much Love to you Always!

To my Sister Keepers, thanks for being listening ears, purpose pushers, and awesome writing adjudicators!

To everyone who pushed me, prayed for me, and doubted me- Thank you!!

THE VISIONS OF THE CLOSED EYED DELICACY

Artist, K. Hardison focuses on the beauty of women who have different lifestyles. She sees herself in a lot of her paintings. They identify areas of her life experience over the past years.

Katrina created closed eyed faces with different emotions. She used watercolor based paint and tempera colors to express each emotion. Purple represents royalty. Red is a symbol of the blood of Jesus.

In her "Closed Eyed" masterpieces, Katrina is able to express the relationship that these women have with God. They close their eyes to remain focused regardless of the distractions in life. Imagine what it would be like to lose focus by always opening the eyes up to allow negativity to overtake your life. The paintings speak life through different colors and allow healing to take place.

K. Hardison
THE VISIONS OF THE CLOSED EYED DELICACY

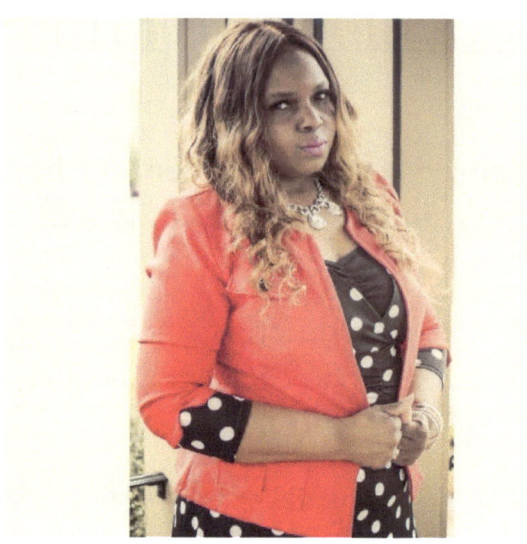

THE ARTIST SPEAKS

Thank you for taking the time to view my masterpieces. God has anointed us with gifts that we must operate in. I pray that as you browse this book that the peace of God will flow within you.

This book is some of my testimony. These paintings are originals that God placed in my Spirit.

Enjoy your journey!

Be Blessed Always!!

K. Hardison

2018

K. Hardison
THE VISIONS OF THE CLOSED EYED DELICACY

NINE BY TWELVE

Artwork dimensions 9 inches by 12 inches

Watercolors and Tempera Paint

K. Hardison
THE VISIONS OF THE CLOSED EYED DELICACY

Broken but Healed, *2018*

"Broken but Healed" contains a lot of brokenness (dark) in her background. She always stays connected to God to help her get through tough situations. Her purple represents Royalty. She is more than a conqueror. This is my first painting.

K. Hardison
THE VISIONS OF THE CLOSED EYED DELICACY

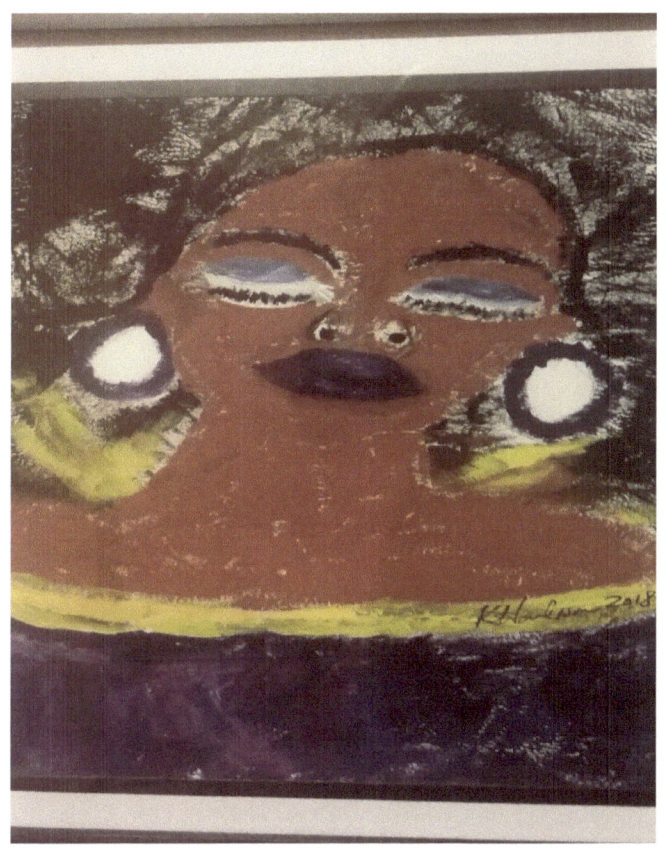

K. Hardison
THE VISIONS OF THE CLOSED EYED DELICACY

The Producer, 2018

Her background is full of brightness. She never allows bad days to stop her. She keeps pressing knowing that blessings are on the way. Pink is her passion. Her lips speak life after the storm.

K. Hardison
THE VISIONS OF THE CLOSED EYED DELICACY

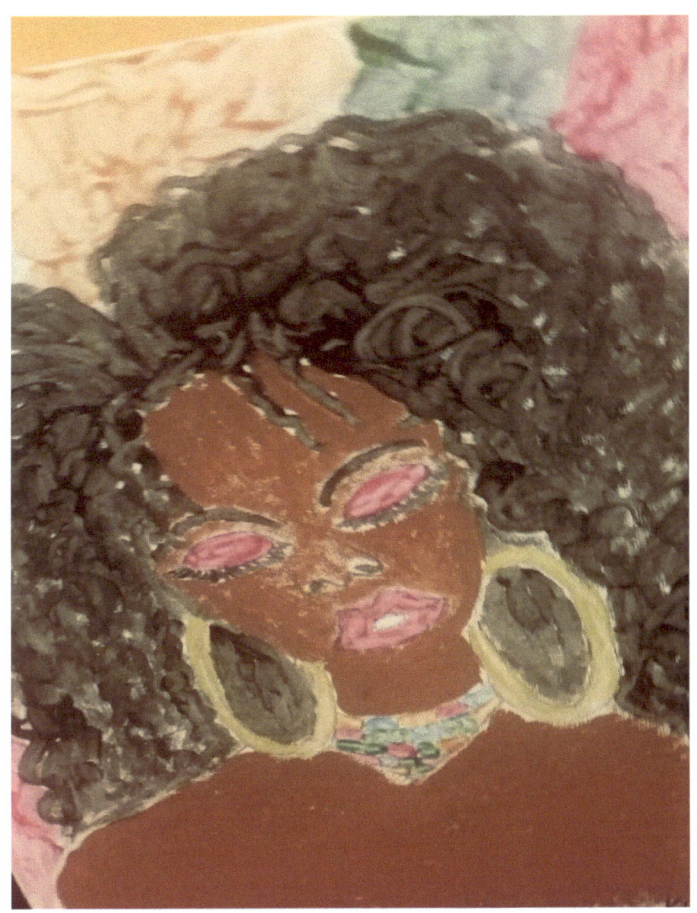

K. Hardison
THE VISIONS OF THE CLOSED EYED DELICACY

One Eyed Elegance, *2018*

Sometimes her identity is mistaken because of her light skin color. She loves a challenge. Her red lips stand for boldness and the covering in the blood of Jesus. Her background is a mixture of gray and black which represents cloudy areas in her life. She is an overcomer.

K. Hardison
THE VISIONS OF THE CLOSED EYED DELICACY

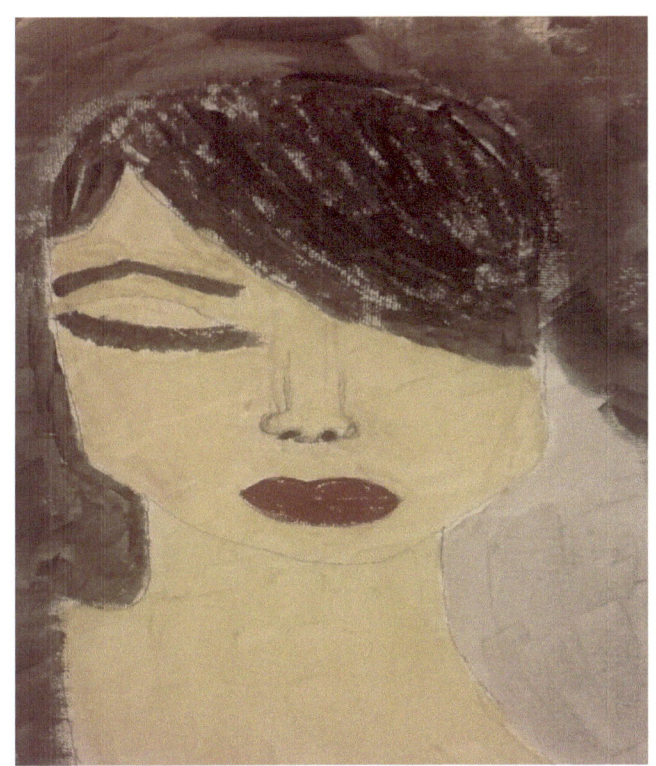

K. Hardison
THE VISIONS OF THE CLOSED EYED DELICACY

My Black is Beautiful, 2018

Her skin is dark brown close to black. She is rejected by many. She has learned to deal with the rejection because she knows who she is. The purple in her eyelashes and sweater symbolizes Royalty. The red symbolizes the blood of Jesus that prevails over all.

K. Hardison
THE VISIONS OF THE CLOSED EYED DELICACY

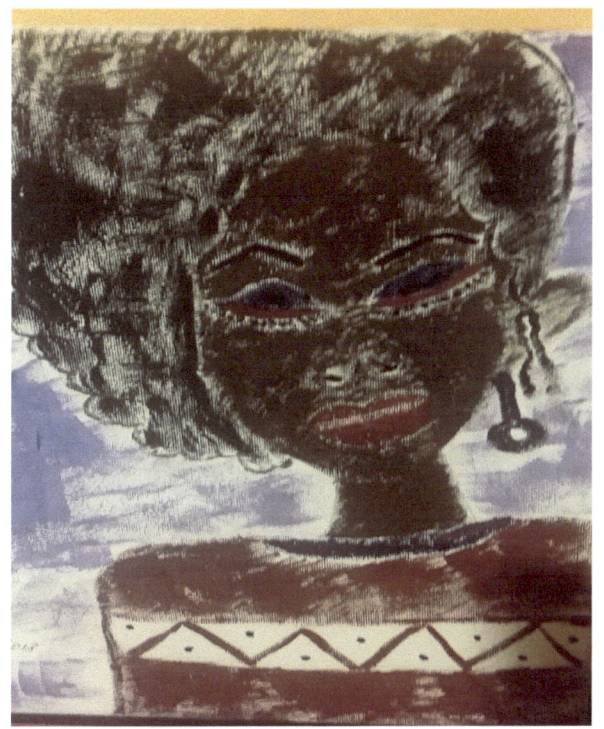

K. Hardison
THE VISIONS OF THE CLOSED EYED DELICACY

Purpose Pusher, 2018

Her caramel colored skin represents a uniqueness. She is one of a kind. She knows who she is and is often misunderstood. She is the "Boss Lady". Her red choker necklace symbolizes the attacks on her life. Her glasses represent the vision that she has which is ordained by God.

K. Hardison
THE VISIONS OF THE CLOSED EYED DELICACY

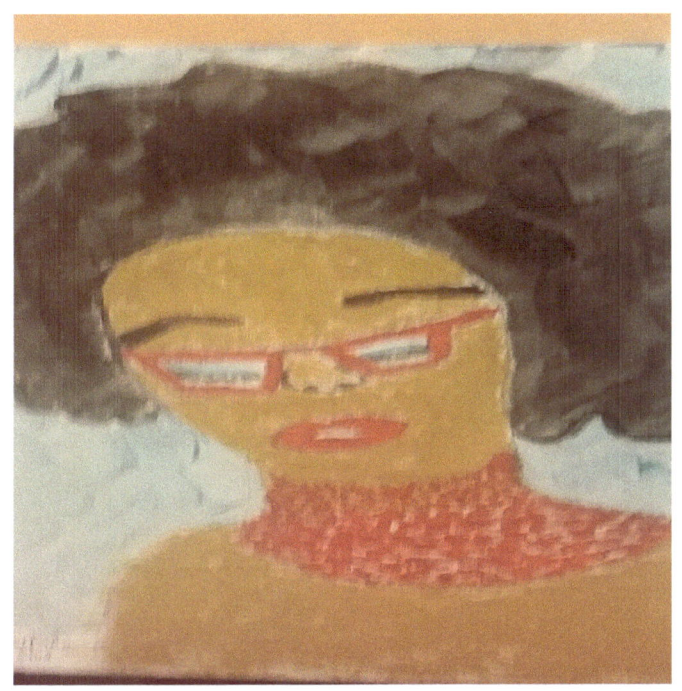

K. Hardison
THE VISIONS OF THE CLOSED EYED DELICACY

Queen of Power, *2018*

This painting symbolizes a Queen who continues to work hard. Her smile says that nothing can stop her flow. The purple represents Royalty. She knows that if she stays in the race that the Victory is hers.

K. Hardison
THE VISIONS OF THE CLOSED EYED DELICACY

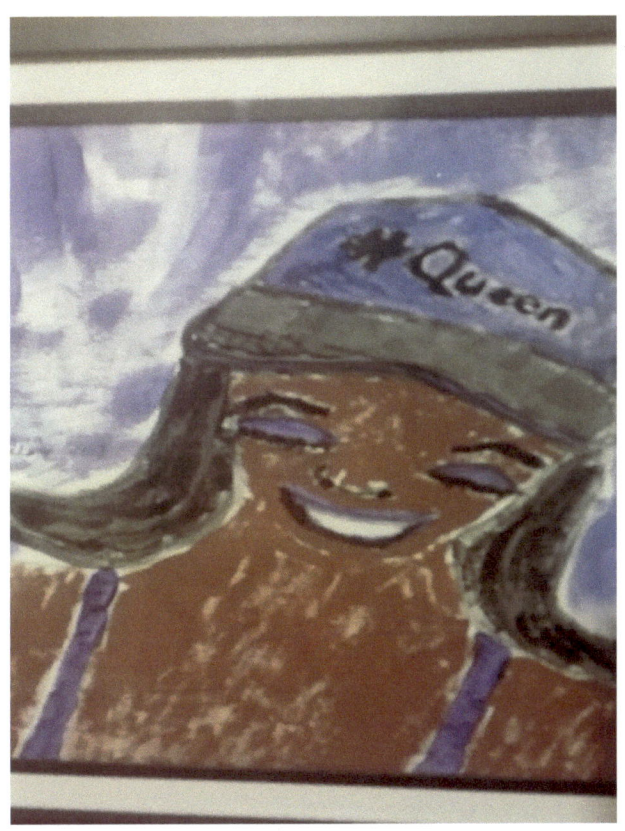

K. Hardison
THE VISIONS OF THE CLOSED EYED DELICACY

Blonde Closed Eyed Cutie, 2018

She represents beauty in her own way. She believes that because she is different and that she is chosen. She is wearing a black dress which represents how darkness tries to overtake her but her faith in God never fails.

K. Hardison
THE VISIONS OF THE CLOSED EYED DELICACY

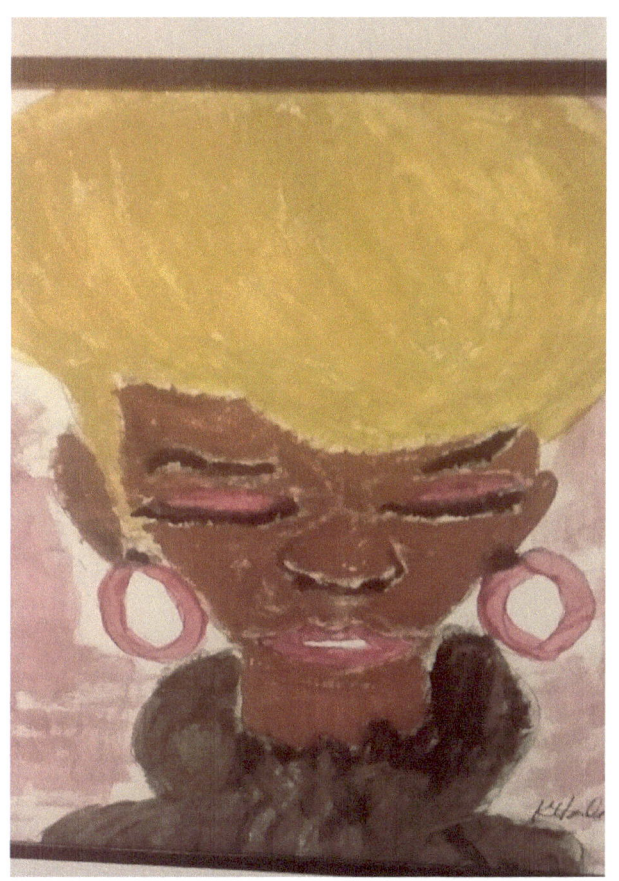

K. Hardison
THE VISIONS OF THE CLOSED EYED DELICACY

Staying in Her Own Lane, *2018*

She loves minding her own business. Her green headphones allow her to flow smoothly regardless of the attacks. She often listens to music which helps her relax.

K. Hardison
THE VISIONS OF THE CLOSED EYED DELICACY

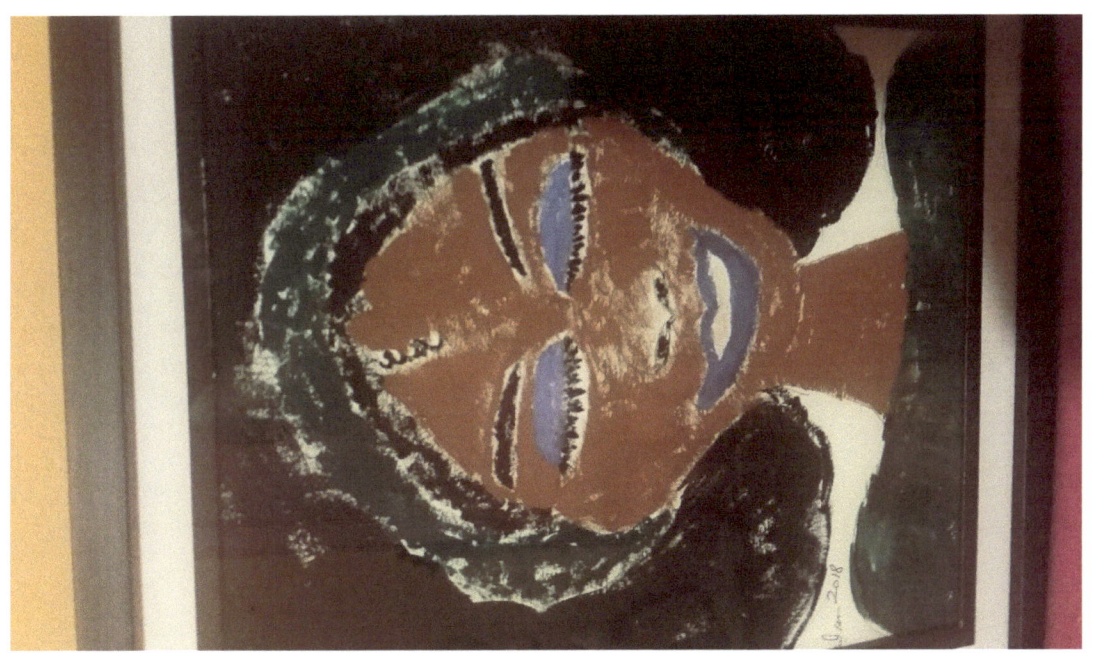

K. Hardison
THE VISIONS OF THE CLOSED EYED DELICACY

Classy with A Little Thug, *2018*

She is one who won't easily break down. She is meek, but not weak. Her headband shows that she is surrounded by temptation but keeps Christ in the center. She chooses to do what's right yet loves a little spice in her life!

K. Hardison
THE VISIONS OF THE CLOSED EYED DELICACY

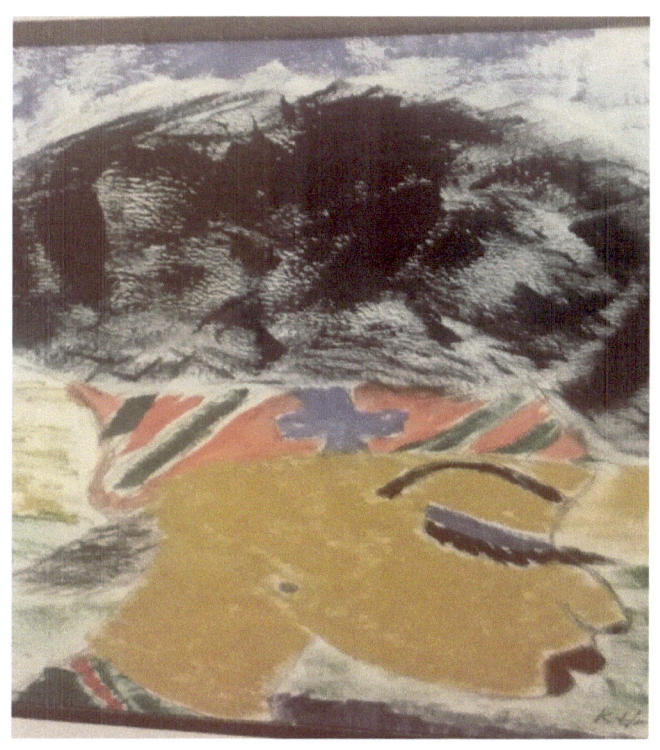

K. Hardison
THE VISIONS OF THE CLOSED EYED DELICACY

Closed Eyed Calmness, *2018*

She remains calm in all situations. She loves to get dressed and go out. She is often faced with trials and tribulations dealing with family members. Her peace is within. She walks in Royalty.

K. Hardison
THE VISIONS OF THE CLOSED EYED DELICACY

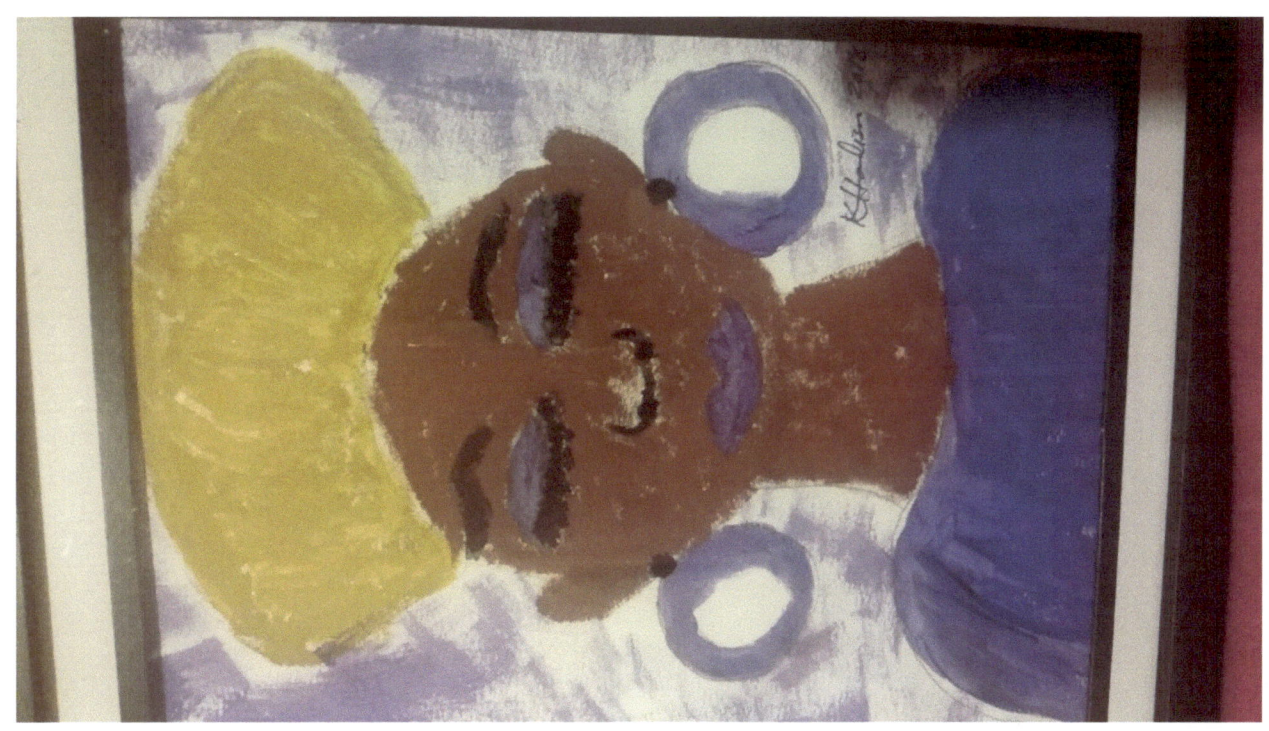

K. Hardison
THE VISIONS OF THE CLOSED EYED DELICACY

Confused, *2018*

She is often confused about her identity. She allows others to dictate to her about life. She is considered a weak vessel. The blood of Jesus keeps her covered (red eyeshadow and lips). She represents Royalty. She is the daughter of a King.

K. Hardison
THE VISIONS OF THE CLOSED EYED DELICACY

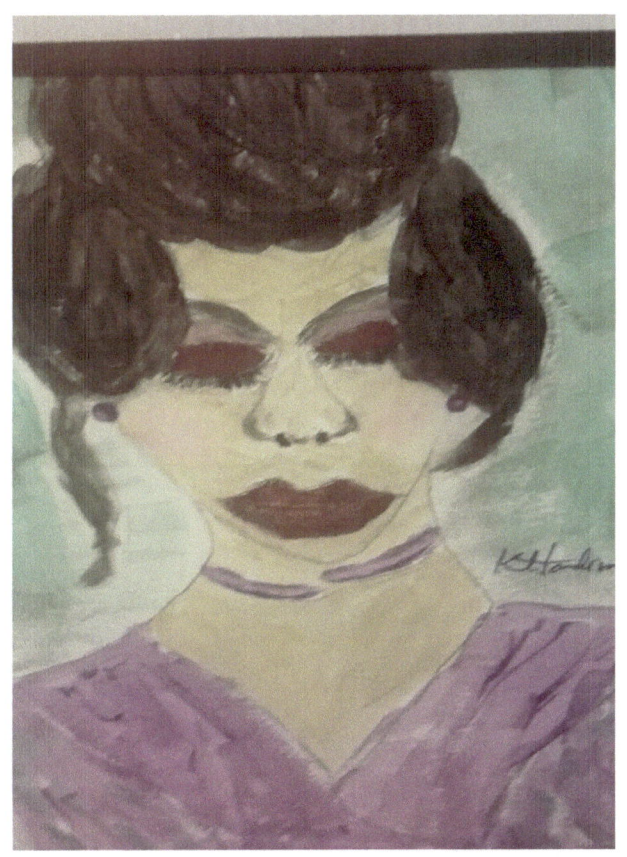

K. Hardison
THE VISIONS OF THE CLOSED EYED DELICACY

Lust or Love, *2018*

She is always searching for Mr. Right. Her hair is always slanted to the side as she feels sexy. She is confused and should not be the chaser but should be chased. Her next chapter will be different.

K. Hardison
THE VISIONS OF THE CLOSED EYED DELICACY

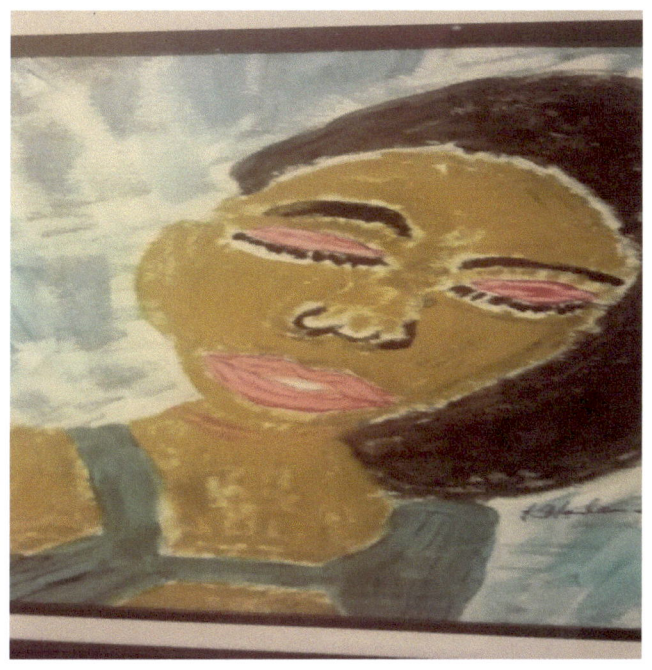

K. Hardison
THE VISIONS OF THE CLOSED EYED DELICACY

Short and Sassy, *2018*

She loves to travel. She stays positive and never loses focus. Her hair is who she became after being healed from a terminal illness. She always encourages others even when she needs encouraging.

K. Hardison
THE VISIONS OF THE CLOSED EYED DELICACY

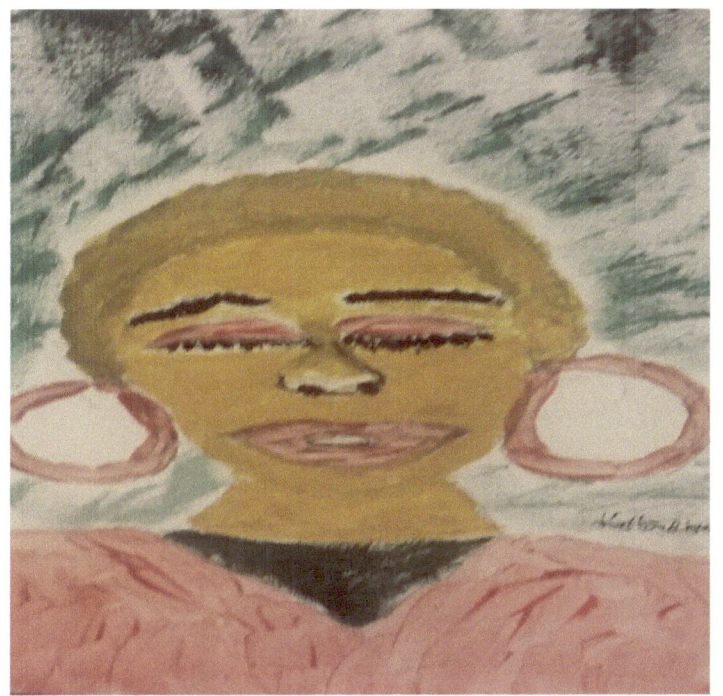

kharrishardison1@gmail.com

K. Hardison

THE VISIONS OF THE CLOSED EYED DELICACY

www.ingramcontent.com/pod-product-compliance
Lightning Source LLC
Chambersburg PA
CBHW051822210526
45473CB00005B/1698